P9-ARQ-285

# The First Book of
# PRESIDENTS

### Revised Edition

*by Harold Coy*

*Illustrated with engravings and photographs*

A First Book

FRANKLIN WATTS | NEW YORK | LONDON

Updated 1981

DISCARD

Hiram Halle Memorial Library
Pound Ridge, New York
10576

1/82   WLS   4 14

J
923
c

42777

*Photographs courtesy of:*
Library of Congress: page 3
National Park Service, U.S. Department of the Interior:
page 16
U.S. Signal Corps, National Archives: pages 7, 14
The White House: pages 9, 63, 64
United Press International, Inc.: 65
Copyright White House Historical Association.
Photographs by the National Geographic Society:
opp. page 1; page 11
All other photographs courtesy of:
Bureau of Engraving and Printing

Library of Congress Cataloging in Publication Data

Coy, Harold.
The first book of Presidents.

(A First book)
Includes index.
SUMMARY: Describes the general duties and
responsibilities of the President and summarizes
the careers of those who have held the office.
1. Presidents—United States—Biography—
Juvenile literature. [1. Presidents] I. Title.
E176.1.C798 1977    973'.0992 [B]    77-1600
ISBN 0-531-02906-9

Seventh Edition
Copyright © 1952, 1961, 1964, 1966, 1969, 1973, 1977, 1981
by Franklin Watts, Inc.
All rights reserved
Printed in the United States of America
10   9

# Contents

*The office of the President of the United States*

## Why We Have a President

Old Ben Franklin was beaming. He had often told the thirteen colonies that they must "join or die." Now, as thirteen independent states, they were joining in a federal union. Franklin, at eighty-one, was seeing his dream come true.

It was September, 1787. All summer, the members of the Constitutional Convention had been meeting in Philadelphia's Independence Hall, planning and arguing.

At last a Constitution had been written. It wasn't exactly what anyone wanted but it was the best they could do. It took a lot of "give and take" to agree at all. The small states were jealous of the big ones. All the states were jealous of the new central government.

To make sure the new government would not grow tyrannical, the convention members divided its power three ways. There would be a Congress to make laws. The courts would say what the laws mean. And someone must be at the head of the government to enforce the laws. This man, the Constitution stated, would be "the President of the United States of America."

## Who Can Be President?

Anybody, so the saying goes, can be President of the United States. Actually this is not quite true. The Constitution says the President must be:

a United States citizen from birth

at least thirty-five years old

fourteen years a resident of this country.

A President serves four years and may be reelected for four years more. A 1951 change in the Constitution provides that no President can serve for more than two terms.

Sometimes the President is spoken of as "the people's choice," but you will not find this in the Constitution. When it was written, few people voted without owning property. Even these voters were to choose only electors for their state. These electors were to pick a President. In practice it has worked out differently.

## How a President Is Elected

Because people have different ideas about government, they separated into political parties early in our history. Soon each party was agreeing on its own man for President, and picking electors pledged to vote for him.

At first the party's members in Congress picked its candidate. Nowadays the choice is made at national conventions.

A man wishing to be President announces that he is trying

*The President's House, Washington, D.C., 1814*

for the office. Then he asks convention delegates to promise their votes to him. At the convention a friendly delegate makes a speech putting him up as the party's candidate for President. Other friendly state delegates march down the aisles, carrying banners and cheering him. Several men are usually suggested as candidates. Then ballots are taken until one man has more than one half the votes. He is his party's choice for President.

Next the campaign for election is on. Each party works for its man, passing out leaflets and staging meetings to tell the voters about him. Each candidate tours the country making speeches outlining what he plans to do if elected.

All candidates appear on radio and television broadcasts.

Election Day is the first Tuesday after the first Monday in November. Soon everyone knows who the President will be. People almost forget that they have really voted for electors from their state. In December these electors meet at their state capital. They vote for their party's Presidential candidate, so he gets all that state's electoral votes no matter how close the race. The electors of all the nation make up the Electoral College. But they never meet as a group. Congress counts the electoral vote in January and announces the name of the next President of the United States.

HOW MANY ELECTORAL VOTES DOES YOUR STATE HAVE?

| | | | | | | | |
|---|---|---|---|---|---|---|---|
| Ala. | 9 | Ill. | 26 | Mont. | 4 | R. I. | 4 |
| Alaska | 3 | Ind. | 13 | Neb. | 5 | S. C. | 8 |
| Ariz. | 6 | Iowa | 8 | Nev. | 3 | S. D. | 4 |
| Ark. | 6 | Kan. | 7 | N. H. | 4 | Tenn. | 10 |
| Calif. | 45 | Ky. | 9 | N. J. | 17 | Tex. | 26 |
| Colo. | 7 | La. | 10 | N. M. | 4 | Utah | 4 |
| Conn. | 8 | Maine | 4 | N. Y. | 41 | Vt. | 3 |
| D. C. | 3 | Md. | 10 | N. C. | 13 | Va. | 12 |
| Del. | 3 | Mass. | 14 | N. D. | 3 | Wash. | 9 |
| Fla. | 17 | Mich. | 21 | Ohio | 25 | W. Va. | 6 |
| Ga. | 12 | Minn. | 10 | Okla. | 8 | Wis. | 11 |
| Hawaii | 4 | Miss. | 7 | Ore. | 6 | Wyo. | 3 |
| Idaho | 4 | Mo. | 12 | Pa. | 27 | TOTAL | 538 |

Each state has as many electors as it has members in Congress, counting its Representatives and two Senators. The District of Columbia is entitled to electors under the provisions of the Twenty-third Amendment to the Constitution.

## Inauguration Day

The President begins his duties on the January 20 following Election Day. At his inauguration in front of the Capitol he rests his hand on a Bible and repeats this oath after the Chief Justice of the Supreme Court:

"I do solemnly swear that I will faithfully execute the office of President of the United States, and will, to the best of my ability, preserve, protect, and defend the Constitution of the United States."

Now he is really President and makes a speech known as his inaugural address. He rides down Pennsylvania Avenue in a big Inauguration Day parade. Crowds cheer to wish him well. The outgoing President sits at his side.

Up through 1933, Inauguration Day was on March 4, for new Presidents could not travel quickly to Washington in the old days. Parades have changed with the times too. In 1861 the Capitol was still unfinished, and the Civil War was at hand. Riflemen on rooftops guarded Lincoln's life. He lived to see the Union saved and the big white Capitol dome in place. It towers over the spot where many Presidents, since then, have sworn to defend the Constitution of a united nation.

## The President Has a Big Job

Nearly three million federal employees look up to the President as their boss. The Constitution places the "executive power" of the government in his hands. He is to "take care that the laws be faithfully executed." He has sworn, at his inauguration, "to preserve, protect and defend the Constitution."

This is a big job, but there is more. The President is Commander in Chief of the armed forces. He may also grant pardons or delay the punishment of convicted persons.

The President makes treaties and appoints ambassadors, Supreme Court judges, and other officials. These things, though, he does with the advice and consent of the Senate. The Founding Fathers, remembering haughty British officials, did not want any man or group to have *too* much power.

Thus the power to make laws is divided between the President and Congress. When Congress passes a bill, the President may either sign or veto it. His veto kills the law unless Congress passes it again by a two-thirds vote.

The President delivers a State of the Union message to each session of Congress, telling of laws he would like to see passed. He may even call special meetings of Congress — but Congress doesn't have to do as he asks.

The President has come to have some powers not described in so many words in the Constitution. Since the rise of political parties, he is usually the leader of the party that elected him. So if this party has the most votes in Congress, he often is able to get his way.

In ceremonies such as welcoming kings or laying cornerstones, the President acts for the nation. He is always in the public eye. The people look to him for leadership in time of trouble. They want action and are impatient if Congress tries to stop the President from taking it. So if the country is at war or times are hard, the President usually has more power than ever. But when danger is over, Congress may want to take some of this power away from him.

*The wireless telephone is demonstrated for President Wilson in 1918*

Nevertheless, the President has a big job. And as living gets more complicated, his job seems to grow bigger.

## He Has a Few Extra Jobs

The eyes of the people are on the President all the time. As the nation's head he proclaims Thanksgiving, asks help for the Red Cross and the Community Chest, and greets an endless flow of visitors. At press conferences the President faces a battery of reporters. Questions come fast and furious. The President has to think quickly — so he won't say something he is sorry for and get into trouble.

## The President Is a Traveling Man

Presidents have always had to travel. Washington, Jefferson, Jackson, and other early Presidents were excellent horsemen from boyhood. They liked to ride horseback except on state occasions or when accompanying their ladies. Roads were poor, and the fine gilded coaches were liable to overturn in mudholes. Even in the streets of Washington, pigs scampered under the wheels.

Steamboats and railroads speeded up Presidential travel. Van Buren came part of the way to his inauguration by train in 1837. Today the President has an armored railroad car with bullet-proof windows, as well as his own automobile, yacht, and plane.

Jet aircraft are at his command. The President can visit a dozen world capitals for talks with leaders of other nations more

*President Johnson conferring with Prime Minister Wilson of Great Britain*

quickly than Washington was able to pay his respects to the town selectmen on a New England tour.

## What Does the Job Pay?

Each year the President's pay checks amount to          $200,000
This is eight times what Washington
got, but prices are higher now. Many
executives and movie stars earn more.

THE PRESIDENT ALSO GETS THESE EXTRAS

| | |
|---|---|
| Taxable allowance for expenses resulting from official duties | $ 50,000 |
| Travel and entertainment, up to | $ 40,000 |
| A furnished house and a country retreat | |
| Counselors, assistants, secretaries, servants | |
| A Secret Service detail to guard his life | |
| A limousine, a yacht, a private plane | |

A lifetime pension of $60,000 a year, up to $65,000 annually for office help, and other benefits
Some expenses still come out of the President's own pocket. A President seldom saves anything from his salary. Still it is an exciting job. Lots of people would like to have it.

## The President's Cabinet

The President appoints trusted helpers to advise him on the nation's affairs. These he calls his Cabinet. They are:

*The Cabinet Room*

THE SECRETARY OF STATE, who deals with foreign countries.

THE SECRETARY OF THE TREASURY: tax and money duties.

THE SECRETARY OF DEFENSE: Army, Navy, Air Force.

THE ATTORNEY-GENERAL, whose Department of Justice enforces federal laws.

THE SECRETARY OF THE INTERIOR: Natural resources, Indian affairs.

THE SECRETARY OF AGRICULTURE.

THE SECRETARY OF COMMERCE.

THE SECRETARY OF LABOR.

THE SECRETARY OF HEALTH, EDUCATION AND WELFARE.

THE SECRETARY OF HOUSING AND URBAN DEVELOPMENT.

THE SECRETARY OF TRANSPORTATION.

Early Presidents had smaller Cabinets, but as the government's work grew, more helpers were added.

## The President's Household

Suppose a million dusty, sometimes muddy, feet shuffled through your home. Your mother would have a bit of tidying up to do. Some years a million people *do* visit the White House. Maids dust the rooms two to three times a day and are forever scrubbing the grand staircase. Keeping 160 windows clean is quite a chore in itself.

To sightseers the White House is a historic spot, to Washington society it is a gay center, and to the President it is a home and an office. No wonder he needs a big household family:

Chefs and butlers for maybe 2,000 dinner guests a year
Housekeeper, chambermaids, ladies' maids, valet
Chief usher, receptionists, telephone operators
Engineers, maintenance men
Gardeners, chauffeurs
A social secretary and a secretary to the First Lady
Secretaries and assistants to the President
A lawyer to advise him
A physician to keep him well
And Secret Service men to guard him wherever he goes.

## The President's Social Life

In the fall of 1951 President Truman entertained Princess Elizabeth of Great Britain. Looking into her eyes, he said:

"When I was a boy I used to dream of a fairy princess. And now here she is!"

It had been 162 years since George Washington became the first President, after winning a war against the Princess's great-great-great-great grandfather, George III. Thirty-two Presidents in that span of time were hosts to many famous folk—Monroe to Lafayette, Buchanan to the future Edward VII of England, Theodore Roosevelt to Prince Henry of Prussia, and Hoover to the King of Siam.

The Princess's royal parents were Franklin D. Roosevelt's picnic guests in 1939 and ate hot dogs. Harding had important guests to breakfasts of hot cakes and sausages. Diplomats dining with Theodore Roosevelt shared the table with baby Quentin in his high chair. The famous visitors from overseas had a glimpse of how ordinary Americans live.

It was once believed that Presidents should imitate the ways of the English court. Washington was expected to bow stiffly without shaking hands. His wife was addressed as Lady Washington.

Jefferson rebelled against this formality, saying a republic should follow simple ways. But Mrs. Madison was too fond of entertaining, and Mrs. Monroe too proud to love simplicity. Mrs. Monroe had so many visitors she couldn't repay social calls—and no First Lady since that time has done so.

Monroe shook hands with all comers. For many years any-

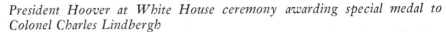

*President Hoover at White House ceremony awarding special medal to Colonel Charles Lindbergh*

body could shake the President's hand on certain days. Hoover put a stop to this tiring practice. It made one's hand too sore.

Home life in the White House is as democratic as in other American homes. But formality in the President's social life is hard to avoid. So many people always want invitations! There are teas, musicales, garden parties, formal dinners, and receptions where diplomats, judges, congressmen, generals, and admirals mingle. State Department experts decide who goes first and who sits where. Formal affairs run more smoothly when there are rules to go by.

## Mr. President

When Washington became President, the Senate debated what to call him. "His Patriotic Majesty" was one suggestion. Another was "His Highness, the President of the United States of America and Protector of Their Liberties." It was finally decided that the most fitting title for the head of a republic was "Mr. President."

The President has his own seal and flag. Army, Navy, and Air Force aides attend him. He receives many honors. For instance, when the President is welcomed aboard a ship he salutes the flag. From the truck at the top of the mainmast flies his own flag. All hands are at salute. The Marine guard presents arms. The boatswain's mate starts piping, and the band sounds off with four ruffles and flourishes. The gun salute begins—twenty-one guns, firing three seconds apart, an impressive mark of respect to a most honored guest.

15

## The White House

In 1947, the floor began to give way under Margaret Truman's piano. The White House was wearing out. Since 1800 thirty-one families had lived there in joy and sorrow. The outer walls were blackened by fire in the War of 1812. The inside had been riddled to make way for water pipes and telephone lines. It was time to rebuild. The Trumans moved across the street to Blair House in 1948. It was 1952 before they moved back. Everything but the outer shell of the House was done over.

The White House has more than a hundred rooms and offices, but it is not a palace. It was built in the taste of a Virginia planter such as George Washington. Famous rooms, like the State Parlors and Dining Room on the first floor and, on the second, the President's Oval Study and the Lincoln Room with its black walnut bed, nine feet long—all have been restored.

## Donkey and Elephant

What would cartoonists do without the Republican elephant and the Democratic donkey? These lively animals stand for the political parties from which our Presidents have come for a century now.

We have had parties ever since Alexander Hamilton and Thomas Jefferson sat opposite each other in Washington's Cabinet and took opposing sides. The followers of Hamilton were Federalists. The Jeffersonians started Democratic Clubs but also called themselves Republicans. So they became known as the Democratic-Republican party.

Later Andrew Jackson's followers took the name of Democrats and had the Whig party for a rival. In 1840, the Whigs scored a victory when they ran the old Indian fighter, William Henry Harrison, against President Van Buren. General Harrison was the hero of Tippecanoe, a famous battle. His party's emblem was a log cabin with raccoons scrambling over the roof.

The present Republican party was formed after slavery became a burning issue. Lincoln's slogan in 1860 was "The Constitution and the Union, Now and Forever." When he ran again four years later, the Civil War was on. Now the cry became, "Don't Swap Horses in the Middle of the Stream."

War memories lasted many years. The Republicans became the "Grand Old Party," or G.O.P. The South voted Democratic for a long time. It was called the Solid South for this reason.

Usually there are two big parties, but "third parties" can bid for the Presidency too. There have been third parties to outlaw liquor or bring about social changes. Theodore Roosevelt left or "bolted" the Republicans in 1912 to run for President as a Progressive under the sign of the Bull Moose.

SOME PRESIDENTIAL SLOGANS

| 1904 | Theodore Roosevelt | The Square Deal |
| 1908 | Taft | Stand Pat |
| 1912 | Wilson | The New Freedom |
| 1916 | Wilson | He Kept Us Out of War |
| 1920 | Harding | Back to Normalcy |
| 1924 | Coolidge | Keep Cool With Coolidge |
| 1928 | Hoover | A Chicken in Every Pot |
| 1932 | Franklin D. Roosevelt | A New Deal |
| 1948 | Truman | The Fair Deal |
| 1952 | Eisenhower | I Like Ike |
| 1960 | Kennedy | A Time for Greatness |
| 1964 | Johnson | The Great Society |

# George Washington

*Born:* February 22, 1732, Westmoreland County, Va.
*Occupation:* Planter, soldier.
*Married:* Martha Dandridge Custis, 1759. *Stepchildren:* Jacky, Patsy. *Adopted children:* Nelly, and George Washington Parke Custis.
*President:* 1789-1797. Elected from Virginia.
*Died:* Dec. 14, 1799, Mount Vernon, Va.

Only George Washington could hold the new nation together, his countrymen said. Always, when there was a hard job, they let George do it. He was a boy surveyor on Virginia's frontier, then a big-boned youth commanding the colony's militia. He rode beside British General Braddock when French and Indian foes shot a deadly fire from behind trees. Bullets pierced his hat and coat. Two horses were killed under him, but Washington mounted a third, keeping his head while others broke and ran. After the tall, handsome soldier married the young widow, Martha Custis, he looked forward to the life of a gentleman farmer. But when trouble came with Britain, Washington was chosen to command the American forces. Eight long years he was in the field. Independence seemed like a lost cause late in 1776.

Then, on Christmas night, General Washington, with a few men and horses, crossed the icy Delaware River and seized Trenton. After the terrible winter at Valley Forge, his persistence won a promise of French help. Finally freedom came. Washington was called the Father of His Country and headed the convention where our Constitution was written. He became the first President . . . the only one who was everybody's choice. Two famous Americans sat in his Cabinet. There they battled. Alexander Hamilton led the Federalists. Thomas Jefferson was to form the Democratic-Republican party. We have had parties ever since.

After two terms, Washington retired, worn out by long service. General, President, Founding Father, he saw thirteen colonies become a free nation. He is remembered as "first in war, first in peace, and first in the hearts of his countrymen."

# John Adams

*Born:* October 30, 1735, Quincy, Mass.
*Occupation:* Lawyer.
*Married:* Abigail Smith, 1764. *Children:*
  John Quincy, Thomas, Charles, Abby.
*President:* 1797-1801. Federalist party.
  Elected from Massachusetts.
*Died:* July 4, 1826, Quincy, Mass.

It was roly-poly John Adams who got the Declaration of Independence passed. To him we owe the festivity of the Fourth of July. He said it should be celebrated by bells and bonfires. And so it has been. Adams, the plowboy, became a famous lawyer. In the Continental Congress, he backed Washington for Commander in Chief.

As President, Adams had many troubles. Some of his enemies were sent to jail, but Americans ever since can criticize even their President. Some of his friends turned against him because he kept peace with France when they wanted war. Yet the new nation kept on going, even with Washington no longer President. Adams lived until July 4, 1826, fifty years after the first Fourth. He was ninety years old. His son John Quincy was now President of the United States.

# Thomas Jefferson

*Born:* April 13, 1743, Shadwell, Va.
*Occupation:* Lawyer, farmer.
*Married:* Martha Wayles Skelton, 1772.
  *Children:* Mary, Martha.
*President:* 1801-1809. Democratic-Republican party. Elected from Virginia.
*Died:* July 4, 1826, Monticello, Va.

Thomas Jefferson declared that all men are created equal. He believed in free schools, religious liberty, and everybody's right to speak his mind. From childhood he loved horses, boats, and outdoor life. His mind, like his body, was active. He watched the stars. He learned how to draw plans for a house, play the fiddle, and read Latin and Greek.

At Williamsburg, Jefferson studied law. He listened at the doorway of the House of Burgesses while England's right to tax the colonies was argued. There he heard Patrick Henry give his clear and ringing speech for the colonies' right to vote their own taxes. From that day, Jefferson was a champion of the rights of America.

At Monticello, Jefferson began a home of his own design. Here, with his wife and children at his side, he tried out new ways of farming, worked on inventions, and read all he could lay his hands on, especially science.

Jefferson wrote the Declaration of Independence. At his urging, Virginia made all churches equal before the law and did away with the custom of property's passing to the oldest son. We owe our money system of dollars and cents to him. Jefferson became Washington's Secretary of State. Later he headed the new Democratic societies of farmers and mechanics.

When Jefferson became President, he walked to his inauguration and had little use for ceremony. Sometimes he received guests in carpet slippers. He was the first President to wear long trousers instead of knee breeches. Sandy-haired and loose-jointed, he stood six feet two. The United States doubled in size when he purchased the Louisiana Territory from France. In his later years, he was proud to start the University of Virginia. Jefferson firmly believed that America would always remain great if Americans were free to seek the truth.

# James Madison

*Born:* March 16, 1751, Port Conway, Va.
*Occupation:* Planter, statesman, lawyer.
*Married:* Dorothea Payne Todd, 1794.
*President:* 1809-1817. Democratic-Republican party. Elected from Virginia.
*Died:* June 28, 1836, Montpelier, Va.

People said James Madison looked like a withered apple. His wife, dark-haired Dolly, sat at the head of the table, always the life of the party. When her shy husband spoke, his voice trailed off to a whisper. Yet "little Jemmy" had a great mind and his own kind of courage. After the Revolution, he worked tirelessly for a Constitution. When one was being written, and he sat below George Washington taking notes, his ideas went into it. So Madison is called the Father of the Constitution. He was President during the War of 1812 and felt the nation's shame when the British came ashore and burned the White House. Soon though, the brave defense of Fort McHenry inspired "The Star Spangled Banner." Two years after the war, Madison returned to Virginia, a neighbor again of Jefferson, the man he most admired.

# James Monroe

*Born:* April 28, 1758, Westmoreland County, Virginia.
*Occupation:* Lawyer.
*Married:* Elizabeth Kortwright, 1786. *Children:* Eliza, Maria.
*President:* 1817-1825. Democratic-Republican party. Elected from Virginia.
*Died:* July 4, 1831, New York City. Buried, Richmond, Va.

Sturdy, blue-eyed James Monroe was old-fashioned enough to wear knee breeches. Born in the same county as Washington, living the same outdoor life, he crossed the Delaware with his commander and received an enemy bullet in the shoulder at Trenton. Monroe's Presidency became an Era of Good Feeling, with hardly an opposing party. England and America disarmed on the Great Lakes. Florida was bought from Spain. The Missouri Compromise brought in Missouri as a slave state and Maine as a free state. The Monroe Doctrine was a warning to Europe to seek no more colonies in the New World. Monroe died just five years after Adams and Jefferson—the third President to pass away on the Fourth of July.

# John Quincy Adams

*Born:* July 11, 1767, Quincy, Mass.
*Occupation:* Lawyer, statesman.
*Married:* Louisa Catherine Johnson, 1797.
  *Children:* George Washington, John
  Quincy, Jr., Charles Francis, Louisa.
*President:* 1825-1829. Elected from Massa-
  chusetts.
*Died:* February 23, 1848, Washington, D.C.
  Buried, Quincy, Mass.

Bald John Quincy Adams, son of our second President, had a cold manner and a warm heart. At seven he had stood beside his mother and watched the colonists fight the redcoats on Bunker Hill. Twice he crossed the ocean with his father to get help for the Revolution. His keen mind was always at his country's service. During his term, roads and canals were pushed into the West. But President Adams' stern appearance won him few friends. Later, as a Congressman, he brought in armfuls of petitions against slavery in the nation's capital. For years, angry lawmakers hooted him down. But Adams insisted that Americans can always ask that wrongs be righted. When the aged man died at his post, he was admired at last for his pluck.

# Andrew Jackson

*Born:* March 15, 1767, Waxhaw settlement on North Carolina-South Carolina border; site claimed by both states.
*Occupation:* Lawyer, soldier, planter.
*Married:* Rachel Donelson Robards, 1791.
*Adopted son:* Andrew Jackson, Jr., nephew of Mrs. Jackson.
*President:* 1829-1837. Democratic party. Elected from Tennessee.
*Died:* June 8, 1845, the Hermitage, near Nashville, Tenn.

Andrew Jackson, first President from the new West, was the son of North-of-Ireland immigrants. He made his way with a strong will and ready fists. The people loved him because he was one of them. At thirteen, he was a Revolutionary soldier. Taken prisoner, he refused to clean a British officer's boots. His punishment was a saber blow, which resulted in an ugly scar on Jackson's high forehead. Under his bristling hair his blue eyes always blazed at injustice. After studying law, Jackson journeyed with a band of pioneers to Tennessee. He helped write the state constitution and argued many a courtroom case. Often frontier arguments were settled with pistols. A bullet missed Jackson's heart only because he was so skinny inside his loose-hanging coat.

In the War of 1812, many Indians took England's side. Jackson rose from a sickbed and waged war to the bitter end against the Creeks. Alabama, their hunting ground, was opened to American settlement. The British felt General Jackson's power at New Orleans. He won a great battle and became a hero.

At his home, the Hermitage, tough "Old Hickory" was the gentlest of husbands. Being elected President was a sad honor when, soon after, his black-haired wife, Rachel, died. On Inauguration Day, men in coonskin caps and muddy boots pushed into the White House to greet their President. Polite society was jarred by their rude manners, but the plain people felt at home. President Jackson battled the Eastern banking interests. He had a showdown with Calhoun of South Carolina over state obedience to federal law, saying: "Our Federal Union—it must be preserved!" It was.

Jackson was straightforward, hating snobbishness and put-on airs. "True virtue," he said, "can only dwell with the people—the great laboring and producing classes." The pioneer Democrat lies in a simple grave at the Hermitage.

# Martin Van Buren

*Born:* December 5, 1782, Kinderhook, N.Y.
*Occupation:* Lawyer.
*Married:* Hannah Hoes, 1807. *Children:* Abraham, John, Martin, Jr., Smith Thompson.
*President:* 1837-1841. Democratic party. Elected from New York.
*Died:* July 24, 1862, Kinderhook, N.Y.

Perhaps Martin Van Buren became President because he was a widower. Jackson's pink-cheeked Secretary of State, with his stylish sideburns, won his chief's heart by paying a courtly call on Mrs. Peggy Eaton, the War Secretary's wife. She was a tavern-keeper's daughter. Cabinet wives snubbed her and made their husbands do the same. Wifeless Van Buren, courteous to this woman of humble birth, became Jackson's best friend and the next President. He first heard political talk at his father's inn. He was known as the "Little Magician" for his skill in politics. But for White House hostess he chose his extravagant daughter-in-law. Gold plates graced her lavish table. When hard times came, Van Buren caught blame aplenty. He wasn't reelected. One woman helped him into the White House. Another helped him out.

# William Henry Harrison

*Born:* February 9, 1773, Berkeley, Va.
*Occupation:* Farmer, soldier.
*Married:* Anna Symmes, 1795. *Children:*
John Scott, William Henry, Jr.
*President:* 1841, one month. Whig party.
Elected from Ohio.
*Died:* April 4, 1841, Washington, D.C. Buried, North Bend, Ohio.

When William Henry Harrison ran for President, a political foe foolishly said he would be more at home in a log cabin than in the White House. He became known as the log cabin candidate—a man of the people. Actually he lived in an eight-room house. He was born in Virginia, son of a signer of the Declaration of Independence, and became first Governor of Indiana Territory. There he met the great Indian chief, Tecumseh, gathering many tribes to fight the white settlers. Harrison parleyed with Tecumseh in vain, then defeated him at Tippecanoe. When the aging soldier headed his inauguration parade thirty years later, he rode into a freezing gale without hat or overcoat. He died of pneumonia after a month.

# John Tyler

*Born:* March 29, 1790, Greenway, Charles City County, Va.
*Occupation:* Lawyer.
*Married:* Letitia Christian, 1813, Julia Gardiner, 1844. *Children:* Mary, Robert, John, Letitia, Elizabeth, Anne, Alice, Tazewell, David, John, Julia, Lachlan, Lyon, Robert Fitzwalter, Pearl.
*President:* 1841-1845. Whig party. Elected from Virginia.
*Died:* January 18, 1862, Richmond, Va.

The first Vice-President to reach the highest office through the death of a President was John Tyler. The lean Virginian was a planter, a lawyer, and a governor of his state. To catch Southern Democratic votes, the Whigs made him Harrison's running mate. But he had a will of his own, and fought for his own way. Soon he was a President without a party. His Cabinet quit, all but Daniel Webster, who stayed on to settle the boundary between Maine and Canada. While Tyler was cruising on the Potomac, a Navy gun blew up. Miss Julia Gardiner, one of his guests, lost her father in the tragedy. But she found a husband and became the President's second wife. Near the close of his term, Texas entered the Union.

## James K. Polk

*Born:* November 2, 1795, Mecklenburg
   County, N.C.
*Occupation:* Lawyer.
*Married:* Sarah Childress, 1824.
*President:* 1845-1849. Democratic party.
   Elected from Tennessee.
*Died:* June 15, 1849, Nashville, Tenn.

When a telegraph message said Polk was the Democratic choice for President, people thought the new invention must be a fake —outside Tennessee he was little known. So Polk became the first "dark horse" to run for President. "All of Texas and all of Oregon" was James K. Polk's slogan. He fought Mexico over the Texas boundary and came out with the Southwest and California too. In the Northwest he settled with England for the present United States-Canadian line. The care-worn President, with so much to put in his diary, wrote it by the new-fangled gaslight before he left the White House. He lived to see the California gold rush begin.

# Zachary Taylor

*Born:* November 24, 1784, Orange County,
   Virginia.
*Occupation:* Soldier.
*Married:* Margaret Smith, 1810. *Children:*
   Sarah Knox, Richard, Elizabeth, Ann.
*President:* 1849-1850, one year, four months.
   Whig party. Elected from Louisiana.
*Died:* July 9, 1850, Washington, D.C. Bur-
   ied, Springfield, Ky.

Zachary Taylor was called "Old Rough and Ready." Forty years
he was a soldier fighting Indians and living in frontier posts. He
won fame as a hero of the war with Mexico. Yet no one looked
less like a soldier. The dumpy, short-legged General had to be
helped to the saddle. As he rode Old Whitney into battle, he wore
a checked gingham coat and battered straw hat. At the White
House, he strolled over the lawn, shaking hands with all comers
while a band played military airs. Though Taylor was a slave-
holder, he swore to defend the Union and hang as traitors any
who took up arms against the federal government. The plain-spo-
ken old soldier suffered a sunstroke while dedicating the Washington Monument and died five days later.

# Millard Fillmore

*Born:* January 7, 1800, Summer Hill, Cayuga County, N.Y.

*Occupation:* Lawyer.

*Married:* Abigail Powers, 1826; Caroline McIntosh, 1858. *Children:* Mary Abigail, Millard Powers.

*President:* 1850-1853, two years, eight months. Whig party. Elected from New York.

*Died:* March 8, 1874, Buffalo, N.Y.

The hot debate over slavery was coming to a boil when Vice-President Millard Fillmore stepped into Zachary Taylor's shoes. The new President, at fifty, could look back with satisfaction on the efforts by which he had risen from a dyer's apprentice to the highest place in public office. As a tall, handsome Congressman, he had been against slavery. Now again he had to make a choice. This time, hoping to patch up the bitter sectional quarrel, he signed the Fugitive Slave Act, forcing return of runaway slaves to the South. This put the North into an uproar. Fillmore was the last Whig President. During his term, Congress voted money to develop the telegraph system. In 1853, Fillmore sent Commodore Perry to Japan to open that far land to the western world.

34

# Franklin Pierce

*Born:* November 23, 1804, Hillsboro, N. H.
*Occupation:* Lawyer.
*Married:* Jane Appleton, 1834. *Son:* Benjamin.
*President:* 1853-1857. Democratic party. Elected from New Hampshire.
*Died:* October 8, 1869, Concord, N. H.

At forty-eight, Franklin Pierce was the youngest man yet to become President. The good-looking New England lawyer was a "dark horse." Like Fillmore and Buchanan, he was a Northerner who favored the South. These men were called "doughfaces." Pierce could be kneaded like dough by his War Secretary, Jefferson Davis, who later became the Confederate President. Southern leaders feared the growth of the North. To keep things even in Congress they wanted more slave states and looked to the western territories to furnish these. Stephen A. Douglas wrote the Kansas-Nebraska Act, allowing the new settlers there to vote on having slaves. Davis took him to the White House to talk to Pierce. Next day the President helped get the new law passed. Soon bloody fights broke out in Kansas. The Northerners complained of unfair help to the slavery group, and themselves hurried reinforcements to their Kansas friends. It was a forewarning of the Civil War that was to come, not many years later.

# James Buchanan

*Born:* April 23, 1791, Franklin County, Penn.
*Occupation:* Lawyer.
*Bachelor.*
*President:* 1857-1861. Democratic party. Elected from Pennsylvania.
*Died:* June 1, 1868, Lancaster, Penn.

While James Buchanan was President, the Union began to fall apart. The powerful-looking man had been Secretary of State and Minister to Britain. But now he was frightened. The Supreme Court said slaves were property even when taken to free states. John Brown tried to start a slave uprising and was hanged. Excitement over slavery was spreading through the land. After Lincoln was elected, but before he took office, South Carolina led seven states out of the Union and sent three men to Buchanan to demand the surrender of Federal forts. "Gentlemen, you don't give me time to say my prayers," the unhappy President told the Southerners. He worried still more when Federal Major Anderson prepared to hold out against the South at Fort Sumter, in Charleston Harbor. Buchanan hoped somehow Civil War could be avoided. As he finished his term, the nation hung on the verge of conflict.

# Abraham Lincoln

*Born:* February 12, 1809, Hardin County, Ky.
*Occupation:* Lawyer.
*Married:* Mary Todd, 1842. *Children:* Robert, Edward, Willie, Tad.
*President:* 1861-1865. Republican party. Elected from Illinois.
*Died:* April 15, 1865, Washington, D.C. Buried, Springfield, Ill.

Young Abraham Lincoln once told a friend, "I have done nothing to make any human being remember that I have lived." He had been a lonely child, losing his mother at nine and working like his frontier neighbors with little chance for school. Every book he could find he read. Young Abe thought a lot as he was growing up . . . and "up" was the way he grew—to a full six feet four. The lean railsplitter was a powerful wrestler. People roared at his funny stories and loved to hear him speak. Once the young frontiersman took a flatboat to New Orleans with goods on board. At a slave auction, he saw a beautiful Negro girl put up for sale. Abe decided then that if he ever got a chance to hit slavery, he would hit it hard.

"Honest Abe" kept a country store and taught himself law. The young lawyer and Stephen A. Douglas both wished to marry

Mary Todd—and Lincoln won. He went to Congress and spoke against the Mexican War. In 1858, he ran for the Senate against Douglas and debated with him over the spread of slavery. This time Lincoln lost.

In 1860, the Republicans put up Abe for President—and picked a winner. Four years of Civil War lay ahead. The Union generals suffered many defeats. Lincoln's own Cabinet was against him. But he struggled on, freeing the slaves and declaring at Gettysburg that government of the people, by the people, and for the people must not perish from the earth. When victory came, and Lincoln walked through Richmond, slaves, now free, kissed his hand. Eleven days later an assassin shot and killed the President who had hoped to reunite North and South "with malice toward none." The Lincoln funeral train moved through a grieving land, back to Illinois. Even many Southerners mourned the man who had saved the Union.

# Andrew Johnson

*Born:* December 29, 1808, Raleigh, N. C.
*Occupation:* Tailor, public official.
*Married:* Eliza McCardle, 1827. *Children:* Martha, Charles, Robert, Mary, Andrew, Jr.
*President:* 1865-1869. Union party. Elected from Tennessee.
*Died:* July 31, 1875, Carter Station, Tenn. Buried, Greenville, Tenn.

It was bad luck for Andrew Johnson to follow a great President. This two-fisted Tennessean's family were uneducated "poor whites" without slaves. His wife taught him to read while he worked at sewing. The tailor became a governor and a senator. He was a Southern Democrat but stuck by the Union and was Lincoln's running mate in 1864. Once Johnson became President, he meant to be boss. So did Congress, with Lincoln gone. Johnson started to set up Southern state governments again. Congress called for Northern control with Negroes voting. The clash of wills caused bitter feeling. Johnson was impeached—accused of misconduct of office—and tried by the Senate. The vote against him came one short of ousting him but left him little power. Later, Tennessee sent her battling son back to the Senate.

# Ulysses S. Grant

*Born:* April 27, 1822, Point Pleasant, Ohio.
*Occupation:* Soldier.
*Married:* Julia B. Dent, 1848. *Children:* Fred, Buck, Jesse, Nellie.
*President:* 1869-1877. Republican party. Elected from Illinois.
*Died:* July 23, 1885, Mt. McGregor, N.Y. Buried, New York City.

Too little push to amount to much, the neighbors said of the freckle-faced boy who fooled around with horses. Shy "Ulyss" Grant didn't seem cut out for West Point, yet he became a fine cavalry officer. In the Civil War, his blows at Vicksburg and Chattanooga wore down the South. In Virginia, as leader of the Northern Army, Grant vowed to "fight it out on this line if it takes all summer." He fought until Lee surrendered, the next spring. It was plowing time so Grant let Lee's men keep their horses.

As President, Grant signed pardons for men of the South. Friends in office took bribes and the honest, easy-going President got the blame. In old age he wrote his life story so Mrs. Grant would have money to live on. He lies in a granite tomb in New York City under his own message, "Let there be peace."

# Rutherford B. Hayes

*Born:* October 4, 1822, Delaware, Ohio.
*Occupation:* Lawyer.
*Married:* Lucy Ware Webb, 1852. *Children:* Birchard, Webb, Rutherford, Jr., Fanny, Joseph, George, Scott Russell, Manning.
*President:* 1877-1881. Republican party. Elected from Ohio.
*Died:* January 17, 1893, Fremont, Ohio.

Rutherford B. Hayes had been a general, a congressman, and Governor of Ohio, mother state of many future Presidents. The 1876 election was close. Samuel J. Tilden, the Democrat, claimed he was robbed of the Presidency by dishonest elections in the South. Hayes soon removed the last Northern troops from Dixie, where they had been stationed since the Civil War. Trade unions were growing. Federal troops were called out during a great railroad strike. Hayes improved Civil Service so more government jobs would go to those best fitted for them. Like Grant, Hayes wore an old-fashioned beard. But the telephone and other modern things were on the way. One day a young White House guest, Thomas A. Edison, showed Hayes his invention, the phonograph.

41

# James A. Garfield

*Born:* November 19, 1831, Orange, Ohio.
*Occupation:* Lawyer.
*Married:* Lucretia Rudolph, 1858. *Children:*
  Harry, James, Abram, Irvin, Mollie.
*President:* 1881, six and one-half months.
  Republican party. Elected from Ohio.
*Died:* September 19, 1881, Elberon, N. J.
  Buried, Cleveland, Ohio.

Like Lincoln, James A. Garfield was born in a log cabin, struggled to get ahead, and died tragically. He left his father's farm to drive mules over a canal towpath. Sometimes the long lines got mixed up with those of teams pulling other boats. Then young Garfield would be yanked into the water to the merriment of passengers and crew. When poor health forced Garfield to seek other work, he prepared himself to be a teacher. In the Civil War he rose to be a general and then entered Congress and finally the Senate. He served only a few months in the Presidency. Office-seekers swarmed into the White House and even stopped his carriage to ask for jobs. It was a disappointed job-hunter who fired the fatal shot at the President. When the wounded Garfield died, weeks later, the nation had stronger reason than ever to believe in a good Civil Service system.

# Chester A. Arthur

*Born:* October 5, 1830, Fairfield, Vt.
*Occupation:* Lawyer.
*Married:* Ellen Herndon, 1859. *Children:* Chester, Jr., Nellie, William.
*President:* 1881-1885, three years, five and one-half months. Republican party. Elected from New York.
*Died:* November 18, 1886, New York. Buried, Albany, N. Y.

Smartly dressed Chester A. Arthur wore side whiskers and spent two hours at dinner. President Hayes once fired him as a customs collector. Three years later, Arthur was President. Nobody thought he would do very well. But the politician turned an able hand to improving the Civil Service. He speeded up mail deliveries. He fixed over the White House and had a rummage sale of stuff from the attic. He started a Navy of steel ships and watched gun drills from his carriage in fashionable Newport. When the Washington Monument was completed, Arthur was on hand to make a speech. People noticed that the jolly President was about as tall as Washington was and much broader.

# Grover Cleveland

*Born:* March 18, 1837, Caldwell, N.J.
*Occupation:* Lawyer.
*Married:* Frances Folsom, 1886. *Children:* Ruth, Esther, Marion, Francis, Richard.
*President:* 1885-1889; 1893-1897. Democratic party. Elected from New York.
*Died:* June 24, 1908, Princeton, N.J.

Grover Cleveland wedded lovely Frances Folsom and was the only President to be married in the White House. He was the only one to come back after four years out of office. And he was the first Democratic President after the Civil War. Even Republicans admired the big lawyer's good government record as Mayor of Buffalo and Governor of New York. He truly believed his own words: "A public office is a public trust." In 1893, bank failures had Cleveland worried. So did his health. This was a secret. If the President were known to be in danger, business might get even worse. So Cleveland stole aboard a yacht in New York Harbor, and there doctors operated and saved his life. Soon the President was sound as a dollar.

# Benjamin Harrison

*Born:* August 20, 1833, North Bend, Ohio.
*Occupation:* Lawyer.
*Married:* Caroline Scott, 1853; Mary Scott Dimmick, 1896. *Children:* Russell, Mary, Elizabeth.
*President:* 1889-1893. Republican party. Elected from Indiana.
*Died:* March 13, 1901, Indianapolis, Ind.

Benjamin Harrison was the last President to wear a beard and the first to sign his papers under an electric light. Growing up in the Ohio River country, he could remember the "log cabin" campaign of 1840, when his grandfather, William Henry Harrison, was elected President. Ben went to a log schoolhouse, then studied law and moved to Indianapolis. He was a Civil War officer, marching through Georgia with Sherman, and later a senator. With his frosty manner, Harrison was not popular. Sometimes he kept visitors standing while he tapped his pencil, hoping they would go. Cartoonists showed him in his grandfather's hat, much too big for him. Yet things did happen. The high tariff Harrison wanted was passed. And the Americas, North and South, met in Washington for the first Pan-American Congress.

# William McKinley

*Born:* January 29, 1843, Niles, Ohio.
*Occupation:* Lawyer.
*Married:* Ida Saxton, 1871. *Children:* Katie, Ida.
*President:* 1897-1901, four years, six and one-half months. Elected from Ohio.
*Died:* September 14, 1901, Buffalo, N.Y. Buried, Canton, Ohio.

During William McKinley's Presidency, the Spanish-American War was fought, and Puerto Rico and the Philippines became American islands. Hawaii also became American soil. McKinley was another Ohio man—lawyer, Civil War soldier, leader in Congress, and governor of his state. Twice he ran for President against William Jennings Bryan, who was asking for more silver money. Plenty of silver would help the Western farmers, said the Democrats. McKinley and the Eastern businessmen wanted to stick to gold. While loser Bryan traveled everywhere, McKinley stayed home, speaking from his front porch. Four years later, with business good, McKinley promised "a full dinner pail"—and won easily. A madman's shot made McKinley the third President of the United States to die by an assassin's bullet.

# Theodore Roosevelt

*Born:* October 27, 1858, New York City.
*Occupation:* Public official, lawyer.
*Married:* Alice Lee, 1880; Edith Carow, 1886. *Children:* Alice, Theodore, Jr., Kermit, Ethel, Archibald, Quentin.
*President:* 1901-1909, seven years, five and one-half months. Republican party. Elected from New York.
*Died:* January 6, 1919, Oyster Bay, N. Y.

Theodore Roosevelt was a city boy with asthma, bad eyes, and a rich father. Yet this sickly child later won fame as a cowpuncher, Rough Rider, and hero of the common people. To conquer his handicaps, Teddy trained in a gym and became a lightweight boxer at Harvard. He set out for Dakota Territory to hunt buffalo and stayed to run a cattle ranch and hold his own in the trigger-happy Bad Lands. It was a real triumph for the "four-eyed tenderfoot." Back in the East as a Civil Service reformer and crime-busting Police Commissioner, young Roosevelt carried his rough-and-tumble ways into politics. When war came with Spain, he was McKinley's Assistant Navy Secretary. Itching for battle, he led a charge of cavalry Rough Riders up San Juan Hill in Cuba. Now famous, he became Governor of New York.

Some politicians called reforming Roosevelt a "wild man" and put him up for Vice-President to get him out of the way. McKinley died, and suddenly the wild man, at forty-two, was our youngest President. Loving the "strenuous life," he opened a trans-Pacific cable and made dirt fly for the Panama Canal.

With a flock of roughhousing Roosevelt children, and a father fond of jujitsu workouts, the White House was a noisy place. "T.R." dazzled visitors with forceful gestures and a toothy grin. "Speak softly and carry a big stick," was his motto. The President battled for meat inspection and pure food laws. He wanted to save the forests and "bust the trusts"—big businesses that had a grip on steel and oil. The diplomats of warring Russia and Japan met on the Presidential yacht. Roosevelt persuaded them to make peace. After leaving the White House, he hunted lions in Africa. Later he ran for President again on the Progressive "Bull Moose" ticket, and lost. It was hard to be merely former President Roosevelt, for "T.R." loved excitement.

# William Howard Taft

*Born:* September 15, 1857, Cincinnati, Ohio.
*Occupation:* Lawyer.
*Married:* Helen Herron, 1886. *Children:*
Helen, Robert, Charles.
*President:* 1909-1913. Republican party.
Elected from Ohio.
*Died:* March 8, 1930, Washington, D.C.
Buried, Arlington, Va.

The first White House automobile had a 332-pound passenger in
William Howard Taft. He ate beefsteak for breakfast, and when
worried, munched salted almonds between meals. For all the merry twinkle in his eye, Taft did worry sometimes. The tariff he
signed to please everybody made few friends. This Yale man who
loved the law was a federal judge at thirty-four. When he was
Governor-General of the Philippines, garden party guests at Malacanan Palace liked their jolly host. Roosevelt liked Taft too and
pushed him for President. Four years later, "T.R." and Taft fell
out. Both ran for President, both lost. In his last days, Taft was
Chief Justice of the Supreme Court—his dream come true. He
would much rather be judge than President.

# Woodrow Wilson

*Born:* December 28, 1856, Staunton, Va.
*Occupation:* Educator, lawyer.
*Married:* Ellen Axson, 1885; Edith Galt, 1915. *Children:* Margaret, Eleanor, Jessie.
*President:* 1913-1921. Democratic party. Elected from New Jersey.
*Died:* February 3, 1924, Washington, D. C.

For twenty years, Woodrow Wilson worked quietly at Princeton University. Suddenly he was governor, cleaning up New Jersey's affairs, then President of the United States. Less than ten years after he stepped off the campus, the whole world was his stage. Streets in many countries bore his name. Pretty girls scattered flowers in his path through Europe's crowded squares.

The future President grew up in Southern parsonages. His father's church did duty as a Civil War hospital and prison stockade. Young lawyer Wilson liked books better than courtroom battles. He taught about good government and became Princeton's president. The Taft-Roosevelt fight that split the Republican vote made possible his election by the Democrats.

President Wilson told Congress face to face what he had to say, instead of sending a message as Presidents from Jefferson had done. He called for a New Freedom, lower tariffs, stronger laws against trusts, and our present Federal Reserve money system. In

1914, Europe became the battleground of World War I. Wilson was reelected in 1916 because "he kept us out of war."

But soon German submarines sank so many American ships that war came anyway. Food and factories were mobilized. Two million American boys served in France. Wilson suggested "Fourteen Points" for a just peace, with people choosing their own rulers.

The President went to Paris for the peace talks. Not all his ideas won out, but he hoped for a League of Nations, to end future wars. Back home many senators were saying Wilson was too proud to take advice. They turned against his plan. While Wilson traveled around the country, pleading for the League, his health gave way. But he remained firm in faith. Some day, he believed, world peace would really come.

# Warren G. Harding

*Born:* November 2, 1865, Corsica, Ohio.
*Occupation:* Editor.
*Married:* Florence DeWolfe, 1891.
*President:* 1921-1923, two years, five months. Republican party. Elected from Ohio.
*Died:* August 2, 1923, San Francisco, Calif. Buried, Marion, Ohio.

No other President had ever won by so many votes as Warren G. Harding. After a big war, it seemed good to go back to better days with Harding. "I don't expect to be the best President, but I hope to be the best-loved one," he said. The easy-going Ohio editor had a word and a smile for everyone. He became a senator and was so popular he was picked to run for President. With his fine, tall figure, he looked the part. In the White House, he was his same smiling self, surrounded by friends he trusted—but shouldn't have. Big oil scandals disgraced some of the men he teamed with, but Harding died before the full truth was known. He was not to be our best-loved President, but the likable newspaperman is more blamed for his friends than for his faults.

# Calvin Coolidge

*Born:* July 4, 1872, Plymouth, Vt.
*Occupation:* Lawyer.
*Married:* Grace Goodhue, 1905. *Children:* John, Calvin, Jr.
*President:* 1923-1929, five years, seven months. Republican party. Elected from Massachusetts.
*Died:* January 5, 1933, Northampton, Mass. Buried, Plymouth, Vt.

Calvin Coolidge, Vermont farm boy and adopted son of Massachusetts, never wasted words or money. A politician, studying his sour face and dry wit, said, "He is like a singed cat—better than he looks." Coolidge went from humble offices to the governor's chair and the Vice-Presidency. As President, he was thrifty as ever. When Britain and France couldn't pay their war debts, he asked, "They hired the money, didn't they?" White House guests might get ice water in paper cups, but business boomed and was glad to "keep cool with Coolidge." In 1927, Coolidge said, "I do not choose to run for President in 1928"—ten words, no more—and went home when his time was up.

# Herbert C. Hoover

*Born:* August 10, 1874, West Branch, Iowa.
*Occupation:* Engineer.
*Married:* Lou Henry, 1899. *Children:* Herbert, Jr., Allan.
*President:* 1929-1933. Republican party. Elected from California.
*Died:* October 20, 1964, New York, N.Y.

Herbert Hoover, an Iowa blacksmith's son, was a mining engineer in faraway places. He became famous for heading relief in Belgium during World War I. Gunners on both sides honored the relief flag on ships with food for the starving. After 1917, Hoover was wartime food boss for the United States. Americans pulled in their belts and "Hooverized"—saved food. He became Secretary of Commerce and finally President. Then business crashed. Troubled years followed. People wanted a daring leader, and Hoover seemed cold and cautious. After many jobs well done, it was his fate to be President at the start of a big depression.

# Franklin D. Roosevelt

*Born:* January 30, 1882, Hyde Park, N. Y.
*Occupation:* Farmer, lawyer, public official.
*Married:* Eleanor Roosevelt, 1905. *Children:*
    Anna, James, Elliott, Franklin, Jr., John.
*President:* 1933-1945, twelve years, one
    month. Democratic party. Elected from
    New York.
*Died:* April 12, 1945, Warm Springs, Ga.
    Buried, Hyde Park, N. Y.

Four times Franklin D. Roosevelt was elected President—more than any other man. He was born in a Hudson Valley mansion, but his New Deal made him the friend of the poor. Every bank door was shut the day he became President in the midst of a business depression. "This great nation will revive," he told the frightened people. "The only thing we have to fear is fear itself."

F.D.R. talked to the people by radio in "fireside chats," calling them "my friends." His New Deal gave old people retirement money, and young people jobs. Farms and homes were saved. When Hitler's Nazis overran Europe, Roosevelt met Winston Churchill of Great Britain on a battleship to proclaim the Four Freedoms—freedom of speech and worship, freedom from want and fear.

F.D.R. grew up around boats and loved them. He was Woodrow Wilson's Assistant Secretary of the Navy, as his distant cousin, Theodore Roosevelt, had been for William McKinley. Young Roosevelt married T.R.'s niece, Eleanor. She became a famous First Lady, going everywhere to see how people lived. The President traveled widely too, flying far to make plans for winning World War II.

Victory was near when the President died. He had taught a nation not to be afraid, as, years before, he had taught himself. Infantile paralysis had left him crippled, but he exercised and swam to health. The man who wouldn't be an invalid became President. A shining example of courage, he walked with braces or whirled his wheelchair about, indoors.

# Harry S. Truman

*Born:* May 8, 1884, Lamar, Mo.
*Occupation:* Farmer, businessman, public official.
*Married:* Bess Wallace, 1919. *Daughter:* Margaret.
*President:* 1945-1953, seven years, nine months. Democratic party. Elected from Missouri.
*Died:* December 26, 1972, Kansas City, Missouri.
Buried, Independence, Missouri.

Harry Truman improved his luck by never knowing he was licked. The country boy with thick glasses commanded a tough battery in France in World War I. His clothing store failed, but he became a senator and helped save millions in Uncle Sam's spending. From the Vice-Presidency he stepped into Roosevelt's shoes and went to Potsdam for talks with Stalin and Churchill. At his grim signal, the atom bomb fell on Japan. The war ended, the United Nations began. But instead of one world of friends, there were two worlds and a "cold war." Experts, doubting that he could steer the risky course, called Truman an "average man" and a sure loser in 1948. He traveled 30,000 miles, speaking to average people at "whistle stops." Their votes elected the plain Missourian to stay on as skipper. Truman had stumped the experts.

# Dwight D. Eisenhower

*Born:* October 14, 1890, Denison, Texas.
*Occupation:* Soldier.
*Married:* Mamie Geneva Doud, 1916. *Son:* John Sheldon Doud.
*President:* 1953-1961. Republican party. Elected from New York.
*Died:* March 28, 1969, Washington, D.C. Buried, Abilene, Kansas.

During Washington's boyhood, the peace-loving Eisenhowers left war-torn Germany for Pennsylvania. Their descendant, Dwight Eisenhower, was to be a famous soldier. He grew up in a little white house in Kansas. West Point was the first stop on his way to the big White House. He won acclaim in World War II, directing the invasion of Europe that led to Germany's surrender.

"Ike," a five-star general anxious to prevent further war, was elected President in 1952 and again in 1956. His goodwill tours included a swing around Asia. Millions cheered him in New Delhi and Teheran. In 1960, he became the first President to pass his seventieth birthday in the White House.

# John F. Kennedy

*Born:* May 29, 1917, Brookline, Mass.
*Occupation:* Congressman, Senator.
*Married:* Jacqueline Lee Bouvier, 1953.
*Children:* Caroline, John F., Jr.
*President:* 1961-1963, two years, ten months. Democratic party. Elected from Massachusetts.
*Died:* November 22, 1963, Dallas, Texas. Buried, Arlington, Va.

A century after his great-grandfather fled Ireland's potato famine and came to Boston, John F. Kennedy went to Congress. Although he was the Harvard-trained son of a family with money and had a flair for politics, his career was no bed of roses. His back, injured in a World War II sea battle, never stopped plaguing him, but he fought for seats in the House and Senate five times and won, beginning in 1947.

During a long convalescence from a spinal operation, Kennedy wrote a book about political courage. *Profiles in Courage* received the Pulitzer Prize for biography in 1957.

In his sixth campaign Kennedy barnstormed the nation by jet plane, debated his opponent, Richard Nixon, on TV, and at forty-three was elected President, becoming the first of Roman Catholic faith. To the world's leaders Kennedy said, "Together we shall save our planet or together we shall perish in its flames." Many joined him in a ban on atmospheric nuclear tests. At home, feeling mounted against racial discrimination, and he championed stronger civil rights laws. On a mission to further goodwill among men he was struck down by an assassin's bullet beside his gracious, attractive wife, whose dignity in bereavement endeared her anew to a sorrowing nation.

# Lyndon B. Johnson

*Born:* August 27, 1908, near Johnson City, Texas.
*Occupation:* Congressman, Senator, rancher.
*Married:* Claudia Alta (Lady Bird) Taylor, 1934. *Children:* Lynda Bird, Luci Baines.
*President:* 1963 — 1969, five years, two months. Elected from Texas.
*Died:* January 22, 1973, San Antonio, Texas.
Buried, L.B.J. Ranch, Stonewall, Texas.

Upon President Kennedy's death, Vice-President Johnson took the Presidential oath at a Dallas airport and hastened to Washington, where he called for "banishing from our land any injustice or intolerance or oppression to any of our fellow Americans, whatever their opinion, whatever the color of their skins." To the world's hardest job the rangy Texan brought his long Congressional experience. He had been a Senate Majority Leader who excelled in the art of give-and-take and getting things done. Colleagues remember him as an outgoing man, giving old friends a Mexican-style bear hug. In 1964, Johnson ran for the Presidency in his own right. He won by a landslide, but the term that began so auspiciously brought heartbreaking problems of racial strife and a bogged-down war in Vietnam. He did not seek reelection in 1968.

# Richard M. Nixon

*Born:* January 9, 1913, Yorba Linda, Calif.
*Occupation:* Congressman, Senator, lawyer.
*Married:* Thelma Catherine (Pat) Ryan,
1940. *Children:* Patricia, Julia.
*President:* 1969–1974. Republican party.
Elected from New York; reelected from
California.

A steep ascent and a dizzy tailspin—that was Richard Nixon's career. After serving in Congress and the Vice-Presidency, he bid for the top office in 1960 and lost by a hair's breadth. In a 1968 comeback, he won the Presidency; then in 1972 he was reelected by a landslide. He is remembered for his trip of friendship to China and for negotiations leading to American withdrawal from Vietnam.

Nixon's second term, opening triumphantly, was a shambles by 1974. Campaign aides confessed having burglarized the Democrats' Watergate headquarters. Tapes of secret White House conversations suggesting a cover-up came to light. After long investigation, the House Judiciary Committee charged Nixon with obstructing justice, ignoring subpoenas, and violating the constitutional rights of various citizens. Faced with impeachment, a Senate trial, and removal from office, Nixon resigned in August, 1974, the first President to do so.

# Gerald R. Ford

*Born:* July 14, 1913, Omaha, Neb.
*Occupation:* Lawyer, Congressman.
*Married:* Elizabeth Bloomer, 1948. *Children:*
Michael Gerald, John Gardner, Steven
Meigs, Susan Elizabeth.
*President:* 1974-1977. Republican party.
Succeeded from Michigan.

Coming to the White House after the nightmare of the Nixon
controversies, Gerald R. Ford said, "Our Constitution works. Our
great republic is a government of laws and not of men." Eight
Vice-Presidents had become President when their predecessors
died. Ford was the first to replace a President who resigned. After
taking office, he pardoned Nixon for any offenses he might have
committed while in office.

Ford bore the handicap of being a non-elected President. He
was at odds with the Democratic majority in Congress, and his
repeated vetoes of legislation made it difficult to fix national policies.
Continuing unemployment and rising prices convinced many it
was time for a change. In his bid for the Presidency in 1976, he
lost to Jimmy Carter.

Conservative in his voting record, Ford served a quarter cen-
tury in Congress and became House Minority Leader in 1965.
In college he was a star center for the Wolverines. Born Leslie
King, Jr., he was soon given his stepfather's name.

# Jimmy Carter
## (James Earl Carter, Jr.)

*Born:* October 1, 1924, Plains, Ga.
*Occupation:* Peanut farmer, Governor.
*Married:* Rosalynn Smith, 1946, *Children:*
    John William, James Earl III,
    Donnel Jeffrey, Amy Lynn.
*President:* 1977—1981. Democratic party.
    Elected from Georgia.

Jimmy Carter was almost unknown outside Georgia. Then after barely two years of campaigning he was President-elect. What drew America to this peanut farmer of the toothy smile and furrowed face? Was it his reputation for integrity and truthfulness and his record as a reform governor of his state, seeking justice for "the poor, rural, weak, or black"? Was it also his proposal to "take a new broom to Washington and sweep the house of government clean"?

Carter plunged into the state primaries. Carrying Florida over George Wallace of the old school, he showed himself a new-style Southern leader. His appeal became national, and he won his party's nomination and then the Presidency.

Ancestors of his have been on Georgia's red soil for generations. Annapolis man, prominent Georgian, successful farmer, church deacon—Jimmy had been all of these. Looking to overcome the consequences of racial discrimination, he once told his adult Sunday School class, "If you have got any hatred left in your heart, get down on your knees."

# Ronald Reagan

*Born:* February 6, 1911, Tampico, Ill.
*Occupation:* Actor, Governor.
*Married:* Jane Wyman (1940—1948).
*Children:* Maureen, Michael.
*Married:* Nancy Davis (1952). *Children:* Patricia, Ronald.
*President:* 1981————. Republican party. Elected from California.

The man who everyone thought was too old and too conservative to be elected president surprised the entire country with his stunning landslide victory over Jimmy Carter. The Electoral College vote gave him all but six states and his tally in the popular vote was 51 percent.

A relative newcomer to politics, Ronald Reagan was 55 when he ran for and won his first elected office: Governor of California, a job he held for two terms. An unsuccessful bid for nomination in the 1976 presidential campaign held up his hopes, but only temporarily.

Reagan's father was a shoe salesman who traveled a lot; it was his mother who kept the family together in the Midwest. Interest in sports and acting combined to give the young Reagan his first job as a sports announcer. In the late thirties, Reagan took a screen test, and as a result he landed a Warner Brothers contract. Thus, the nation's fortieth president is the first to have been a popular star in Hollywood and on TV. Also, he is the first president who has been divorced.

In the late forties, Reagan's ability as an administrator was tested when he became president of the Screen Actors Guild. After his movie career was over, Reagan used his talents as a perfomer in a new way: he became a public relations executive for General Electric. From there it was only a short step to the Governor's mansion in Sacramento and on to the White House.

# Index